Incredible Explorers

Henry Hudson
Exploring the Northwest Passage

Jack Connelly

Cavendish Square

New York

Published in 2015 by Cavendish Square Publishing, LLC
243 5th Avenue, Suite 136, New York, NY 10016

Library of Congress Cataloging-in-Publication Data

Connelly, Jack.
Henry Hudson : exploring the northwest passage / Jack Connelly.
pages cm.
Includes index.
ISBN 978-1-50260-127-8 (hardcover) ISBN 978-1-50260-128-5 (ebook)
1. Hudson, Henry, -1611—Juvenile literature. 2. Explorers—America—Biography—Juvenile literature. 3. Explorers—Great Britain—Biography—Juvenile literature. 4. America—Discovery and exploration—British—Juvenile literature. 5. Northwest Passage—Discovery and exploration—English—Juvenile literature. I. Title.

E129.H8S55 2015
910.92—dc23
[B]

2014025532

Editor: Andrew Coddington
Copy Editor: Cynthia Roby
Art Director: Jeffrey Talbot
Designer: Douglas Brooks
Senior Production Manager: Jennifer Ryder-Talbot
Production Editor: David McNamara
Photo Researcher: J8 Media

The photographs in this book are used by permission and through the courtesy of: Cover photo by Serverino Baraldi/The Bridgeman Art Library/Getty Images; Boat Seal by Vector Lady; © North Wind Picture Archives, 4–5; Stock Montage/Archive Photos/Getty Images, 7; Print Collector/Hulton Archive/Getty Images, 12; Print Collector/Hulton Archive/Getty Images, 13; Charles Eamer Kempe/File:RichardHakluyt-BristolCathedral-stainedglasswindow.jpg/Wikimedia Commons, 15; British Library/Robana/Hulton Fine Art Collection/Getty Images, 18; Serverino Baraldi/The Bridgeman Art Library/Getty Images, 20; Theodore de Bry/The Bridgeman Art Library/Getty Images, 21; Time Life Pictures/The LIFE Picture Collection/Getty Images, 22; British Library/Robana/Hulton Fine Art Collection/Getty Images, 25; Hulton Archive/Getty Images, 28; www.geheugenvannederland.nl (http://www.geheugenvannederland.nl/?/nl/items/MAU01:8)/File:The dock of the Dutch East India Company at Amsterdam.jpg/Wikimedia Commons, 30; Ambient Images Inc./SuperStock, 34; Stock Montage/Archive Photos/Getty Images, 37; © North Wind Picture Archives, 38; SuperStock/Getty Images, 40; © North Wind Picture Archives, 41; Henry Hudson being set adrift (gouache on paper), Jackson, Peter (1922-2003)/Private Collection/© Look and Learn/Bridgeman Images, 47; Wolfgang Kaehler/LightRocket/Getty Images, 54; Tate, London, 2011/File:John Collier - The Last Voyage of Henry Hudson - Google Art Project.jpg/Wikimedia Commons, 57.

Printed in the United States of America

Contents

Reaching Asia via the North

A s students of history know, when Christopher Columbus found himself in the New World in 1492, he was looking for a new travel route to Asia, and instead landed on two continents previously unknown to the nations of Europe.

While the Europeans looked to settle this new land and exploit its rich resources, the search continued for a direct water route to Asia. Many English explorers looked to take a northern approach, believing there would be an ice-free path to India and China.

The cold Arctic seas took their share of casualties. John Cabot's crew would **mutiny** in 1509 instead of traveling further, and Sir Hugh Willoughby and his team perished in the frigid waters of Norway. John Davis, Martin Frobisher, and William Barents were three additional explorers who failed in attempts to find the **Northwest Passage** to Asia.

While they were unsuccessful, their travels led to a greater understanding of the land in modern-day Canada and the northeastern corner of the United States. They also did not discourage Henry Hudson, who made four voyages to find the

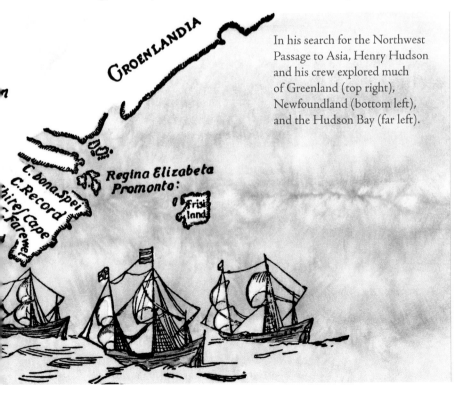

In his search for the Northwest Passage to Asia, Henry Hudson and his crew explored much of Greenland (top right), Newfoundland (bottom left), and the Hudson Bay (far left).

elusive Northwest Passage, and while he did fail in his primary goal, his crews managed to discover the U.S. river and Canadian bay that bear his name to this day.

The maps used by sixteenth- and seventeenth-century navigators, as fantastic as they were factual, provided little information. The dark Arctic seas were clouded by a thick mist and deep fog, so dense in places that guiding a vessel through passing icebergs frequently spelled disaster. Moreover, a compass was somewhat unreliable in Arctic waters because of the close proximity of the magnetic North Pole. (The compass needle points farther away from the geographic North Pole by degrees the farther north you travel. This occurs because the Earth's lines of magnetic force actually point downward closer to the poles, causing a compass needle to read inaccurately.) Other aspects of the journey were unsettling, too, such as witnessing what some sailors believed were sea monsters skillfully gliding past their small wooden vessels.

These dangers associated with exploring a new region were added to the typical problems sailors faced in that era. They included living in cramped conditions, terrible food lacking basic vitamins and nutrients, squalor, diseases, and constantly keeping their ship in proper condition and on course. However, all of these negatives were not enough to prevent English explorers such as Hudson and his countrymen from risking their lives, and the lives of their crew, to discover the possibly rich trade routes of the Atlantic and the rewards they could provide. While they never found that direct route, these explorers provided their sponsoring nations with some of the earliest maps and details of North America, giving the countries the information needed to settle this new world.

Chapter 1

An Age
of Exploration

As the Spanish colonized and dominated the Indies and the southern portion of North America, Henry Hudson became obsessed with finding a direct sailing route to Asia through the icy waters of the Arctic Ocean. Hudson

Henry Hudson was born northwest of London in the sixteenth century during the great Age of Exploration.

would make voyages sponsored by both the English and the Dutch. His explorations of the Hudson River Valley would lead the Dutch to their colonization of the area and the founding of New York City, originally known as New Amsterdam. The details of his voyages are remembered to this day, but little is known about his birth and early life. In fact, there is no consensus about the day or year of his birth.

Hudson was born in England, possibly in the town of Hoddesdon, which is in Hertfordshire County, just northwest of London. Hudson may have been born on September 12, 1570, during the reign of Queen Elizabeth I, in the period known as the **Elizabethan Era**, although few records from this time in history remain regarding Hudson. In fact, scholars aren't even certain of the names of Hudson's parents.

Record keeping during the reign of Queen Elizabeth wasn't centralized or controlled. This resulted in a lack of information regarding Henry Hudson's birth, a fairly common condition in that period. Even standardized spelling, which to anyone today seems routine, was inconsistent at the time. William Shakespeare, for instance, who was Hudson's contemporary, spelled his own name several different ways on various documents. There are documented records of numerous spellings, including Shakespeare, Shakespear, Shackspeare, and even Shake-spear.

There was a good reason for the lack of standardized spelling: In the sixteenth century, the majority of people were still unable to read, so rules of spelling were less important than they are today. Once literacy rates rose to include most people, a standardized form of spelling became more relevant so that readers could understand exactly which words they were reading.

Hudson's family tree provides little more than minor clues about his history. Since there may have been several men who had the first name of "Henry," it's also difficult to understand. Hudson's grandfather, for instance, who was probably a London alderman (councilman), was named Henry Hudson, and there's some evidence that "Henry" might have been Hudson's father's first name as well. Henry the explorer was one of five sons; his brothers were named Christopher, Thomas, John, and Edward.

Unfortunately, personal facts about Henry Hudson are frustratingly few. We're not even sure what Hudson looked like, since the only portraits of him were made long after his death, the date of which is also a mystery. We do know he disappeared in 1611, and that his family owned a townhouse in London. Since his family was involved in international trade, Hudson must have spent at least some of his early years in that bustling city.

London would have been an exciting place to live. Its crowded sixteenth-century cobblestone streets would have been alive with the shouts of merchants and the new plays of Shakespeare and other dramatists. London's first theater opened in 1576, even though outbreaks of plague often closed public gatherings. London was heavily and densely populated at the time, a fact that lent itself to the spread of plague and contributed to the estimated 20,000 lives that were lost there to the disease during the sixteenth century. Like many other European cities, London was also buzzing with plans for future exploration and trade.

The four voyages of the Italian explorer Christopher Columbus to the West Indies years before (1492–1504) had proven that there was more to the world than the English had dreamed. After Columbus, John Cabot (1497), and Sir Humphrey Gilbert (1578–1583) had separately explored the coast of North America and claimed land for England. (John Cabot's son Sebastian was actually the first explorer to search for the elusive Northwest Passage for Spain in 1508.)

The English seafarer Sir Francis Drake (1577–1580) excited all of England when he became the first English explorer after the Spaniard Ferdinand Magellan (1519–1522) to successfully **circumnavigate** the world.

Under the strong leadership of Queen Elizabeth I, England had grown stronger, thriving on trade with the East Indies and Russia. In fact, Hudson's grandfather, the earlier Henry Hudson, was one of the founders of the Muscovy Company, which had made the first contacts with the Russian capital, Moscow, along with Sebastian Cabot.

The young Hudson would almost certainly have been surrounded by talk of adventure and foreign travel. He would have soon been fascinated by what was to become his lifelong obsession, too, which was the search for what would later be officially called the Northwest Passage. This was a conjectured waterway that was hoped to stretch either across the North Pole or (as later explorers would hope) across North America to Asia.

The search for the Northwest Passage might sound unusual in today's world, which relies upon modern maps that are accurate to the smallest detail. Although England had accurate maps of Europe and Asia, neither the Arctic nor the New World had yet been fully mapped. No one had been able to sail to the northernmost regions to see if there was open water or solid land there. Such major rivers as the Saint Lawrence in Canada had been explored, but no one yet knew how far they flowed, or how far inland they could be navigated.

Without a Northwest or Polar Passage, the only way to get to Asia was either by a long, dangerous, and expensive journey east by land, or by a shorter, but certainly just as dangerous, journey by sea. The sea route ran down the African coast, around the Cape of Good Hope, which was the stormy, treacherous tip of South

Africa, then east across the Indian Ocean. The sea journey took months, and between the perils of terrible weather and piracy, many ships never returned. Portugal had also laid claim to this route, another fact that dissuaded exploration of the waters.

The alternate route, which was proved possible by Sir Francis Drake's circling of the world, was longer, more expensive, and even more dangerous. It meant sailing across the Atlantic Ocean, which could take more than six weeks, down around Cape Horn (the storm-racked tip of South America), then out over the Pacific Ocean, which could take twice as long. In short, it would save a great many lives, as well as much money and time, if someone could discover a clear sailing route from England that ran straight across to Asia.

The search for the Northwest Passage was especially important for England since it was fighting an economic battle with the Spanish, the Portuguese, and the Dutch. By providing the country with the safety of a Northwest Passage to Asia, any explorer would drastically improve his country's economic status and expedite direct trade with Asia.

Watching his older brothers and cousins setting out on their journeys, Hudson probably looked forward to his own voyages of exploration. These would have most likely begun in his teens or earlier. Being part of a seafaring family, especially one that made its livelihood from trading, Hudson would have served aboard his family's wooden vessels.

Sixteenth-century English ships had three masts and carried up to six triangular sails. A ship's **prow**, or front, would have been a boxy-looking **carrack** prow, and the **stern** would have had a raised **sterncastle**, or two-story cabin. With only wind to power their ships, they would have been utterly dependent on weather conditions to determine speed.

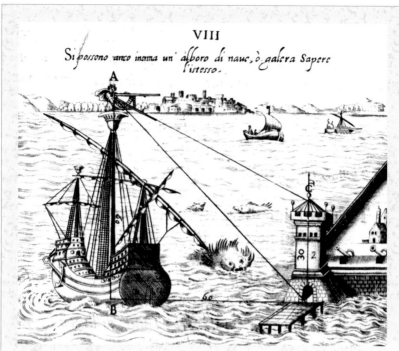

One of the many devices early explorers used to navigate was the quadrant, which could be used to determine a ship's latitude or distance from the shore.

SIXTEENTH-CENTURY NAVIGATION TOOLS

As English ships sailed previously uncharted seas, navigation became an even more important skill for sailors. The basics of using the positions of stars, planets, and the moon had been used since ancient times, but astronomy and mathematics became even more important in the early years of the sixteenth century. A **cross staff**, **quadrant**, or **astrolabe** would measure the angle between the North Star and the horizon, giving the user his latitude. The rocking of the ship or the North Star being obscured by clouds could make the exact measurement of latitude problematic, and being off even a little bit could have drastic effects on a ship's position. In addition, a magnetic compass was a key tool on every ship.

Although Hudson's sailing career began early, it is unclear whether or not Henry Hudson played a role in the defeat of the Spanish Armada, which attacked England in the hopes of removing Queen Elizabeth I from the throne.

Hudson most likely began his career as a **cabin boy**, an aide to the ship's captain. He would have learned navigation by cross-staff and compass, or sailing by the stars and primary directions. Although other instruments were also available at the time, such as the astrolabe and the quadrant, most sailors agreed that those were among the most uncertain. This included John Davis, an English seaman who searched for the Northwest Passage in 1585, some years before Hudson did. He wrote about contemporary navigational instruments in his book *Seaman's Secrets*, an account of which is described in a modern book by Samuel Eliot Morison, *The European Discovery of America*. In addition, Hudson would have been skilled at methods of managing sails, cooking, and reading the weather. He was also literate, since he would have been expected to someday captain his own ship and keep its **log**.

It is unclear what Hudson did in his teenage years, as crew records from the era ranged from scant to nonexistent. Hudson might have been part of the crew that accompanied John Davis on his 1587 journey to discover a direct route to Asia. The fact that Davis planned his journey in the presence of Hudson's brother increases the likelihood of Henry's participation, but it remains speculation to this day. Another area of uncertainty is whether Hudson was part of England's stunning 1588 naval victory over the Spanish Armada, a fleet of more than ten dozen ships that sailed to England with the goal of conquering England and deposing Queen Elizabeth I. Hudson was certainly old enough to participate in either or both, but his name does not appear until years later (1607), when he emerges as a new explorer.

Reverend Richard Hakluyt (left) was one of the early supporters of Hudson's voyages.

Chapter 2

A Frozen Barrier

In 1607, Henry Hudson led his first expedition to discover a northern passage to Asia via the North Pole. Chartered by the Muscovy Company, Hudson captained the *Hopewell* (occasionally listed as the *Hope-well*) on the recommendation of Muscovy board member

Reverend Richard Hakluyt. The reverend, also a geographer, supported Hudson as a captain because he believed that Hudson had key information on finding the long-sought passage to Asia.

Hakluyt (1552–1616) was both an ordained English minister and a noted geographer who was fascinated by the topic of exploration, particularly by the English. He wrote several books on the subject, including *Principal Navigations*, as well as articles to promote the idea of English colonies in North America.

Historians believe that Hudson developed the idea of English colonies in North America from a pamphlet titled "Thorne's Plan," written and published by Robert Thorne in 1527. In it, Thorne confidently wrote that it would be possible to sail due north, over the North Pole, to Asia.

EXPANDING ELIZABETHAN ENGLAND

Hudson's champion on the Muscovy board of directors, the Reverend Richard Hakluyt, was also a fierce proponent for the English colonization of the New World. Hakluyt believed that the settlement of North America would allow the expansion of Protestantism, provide raw materials for England, and give England a place to send its poor and criminal subjects, all of which would expand the nation's economic power. Hakluyt wrote several books on the subject, most notably *Principall Navigations, Voiages*, and *Discoveries of the English Nation*. In addition, he would go on to be an investor in the Virginia Company of London.

Hudson, by this point, was married to a woman named Katherine, though her maiden name and the date of their wedding remain unknown. The couple had three sons, named John, Richard, and Oliver, but again, the records pertaining to these events are scarce. We do know that Hudson took John, who was then about fifteen or sixteen years of age, on the voyage with him. All told, the crew on Hudson's first trip numbered between twelve and fifteen.

> ## THE FROZEN LAND OF THE ARCTIC
>
> Sixteenth-century scientists theorized that the North Pole must be liquid, not solid land or ice. They came to this theory because of their belief that the northernmost Arctic was clear of cloud cover and was warmed by constant sunshine.
>
> Today, scientists know that the Arctic is a solid mass of ice and does not provide a direct water route to Asia. However, jets can fly over the North Pole and reach their Asian destinations far more quickly.

There was a delay in sailing due to bad weather. At last, as Hudson himself records in his journal, "The first of May 1607, we [weighed or raised] anchor at Gravesend and were off."

The *Hopewell*, which was a bark—a ship with two main masts and a smaller foremast (front mast)—sailed north by northwest throughout May without Hudson finding anything of note to record, except the ship's daily position. He also noted a brief alarm on May 30 when the needle on the ship's compass wavered.

That Hudson brushes off so startling an occurrence with only a brief mention hides the fact that there might have been considerable panic aboard the *Hopewell*. After all, this was an age when educated men still firmly believed in demons and ill omens. Something as fixed as a compass suddenly turning unreliable, even briefly, must have been terrifying. It might even have led to the first time that Hudson had to control an attempt at mutiny.

The voyage resumed without conflict. By June 11, Hudson sighted six or seven whales near the ship. Whales in that region would have had no reason to fear the *Hopewell*. They might never have even seen a ship. Unfortunately, this was soon to change, when whaling began in earnest only a few years later.

Finally, on June 13, Hudson caught sight of land. It was the coast of Greenland, already known to geographers but not completely mapped. The *Hopewell* sailed up the coast, heading northeast, through the end of June. Heavy wind, ice, and snow, mixing with unexpected milder patches of warmth and days of blinding fog, marked the voyage. The crew, though somewhat prepared for these conditions with heavier clothing, felt the journey was an unpleasant one. They must have been frightened or just plain miserable, forever damp and chilled. They must have also wondered why Hudson continuously sailed blindly through perilous, unknown waters, when they only wanted to end the voyage.

Early sea voyages were extremely dangerous. Explorers such as Hudson were traveling into unknown waters, and sailors feared that a storm—or a sea monster— might not be far off.

A Brief Improvement of Conditions

By June 23, to everyone's relief, the weather cleared enough for Hudson to sail northeast from Greenland to what he named "Newland," now known as Spitsbergen in the Svalbard Islands, belonging to Norway. Presumably everyone on board the *Hopewell* was feeling more confident at this point, because up until then, the journey was entirely on the open ocean, a fact that gave Hudson great hope about finding the northern sea route to Asia. Since the crew could see where they were going, it's possible that they were sharing some of that hope, too.

The optimism ended when there turned out to be too much solid ice for the *Hopewell* to continue due north. Instead, Hudson and his men explored what must have seemed to be a confusing mass of islands and icebergs.

On July 1, to everyone's relief, the *Hopewell* reached a large inlet of open water, a rich green place full of seals and walruses. However, those high spirits were short-lived, once again. Within the span of ten days, Hudson noted that several members of his crew had become sick after eating spoiled bear meat.

Afterward, they were beset by fog once more. Hudson stated in his journal that a strong wind, or a small gale as he called it, finally delivered the vessel, pushing the *Hopewell* free of fog and ice at the same time. The men's spirits must have been raised when they came to what was to be called Whale Bay, after the many pods of whales they found in it. It is now known as Collins Bay and is situated 750 miles (1,207 kilometers) north of the Arctic Circle.

Some of Hudson's crew, led by his first mate, John Coleman, were able to land on Northeast Land, the northernmost island of the Svalbard Islands that Hudson and his men were exploring. There they were able to hunt game. Fresh meat must have tasted

Whale Bay (modern-day Collins Bay) was named after the many pods of whales that Henry Hudson encountered there.

wonderful to men who had been mostly eating salted provisions they'd brought with them. They were also able to refill the ship's casks with freshwater since chunks of ice brought aboard the ship were suitable for drinking; surely this was among the only advantages to northern exploration.

The *Hopewell* was now about 700 miles (1,126 km) north of the Arctic Circle and in growing danger of colliding with passing icebergs. The ship nearly became a casualty when an iceberg almost collided with it, but Hudson quickly **steered** the *Hopewell* south, and saved everyone.

Hudson accepted the inevitable. It was now the end of August, and the conditions were extremely foggy, wet, and harboring a biting cold. There would be little safe time left for

When the *Hopewell's* supplies began to run low, several members of Hudson's crew disembarked on the Northeast Land, one of the Svalbard Islands, to hunt game and replenish the ship's stores.

exploration. Rather than risk the lives of his men and himself, he ordered them to continue sailing southward toward England. Hudson wrote in his journal: "I hoped to have had a free sea between the land and the ice ... I think this land may be profitable to those that will adventure it."

While Hudson had not found his passage, his commentary would prove farseeing—England would serve as the first nation to take advantage of the financial windfall of whaling based on the information Hudson collected in his first voyage of three and a half months. In the meantime, Hudson had returned his ship and his crew safely to England. He would not be satisfied to remain in England long—he was obsessed with finding the Northwest Passage, and would be ready for a second voyage soon.

Chapter 3

Hudson's Second Voyage

While Hudson had not provided the Muscovy Company with their new shipping route, the company was encouraged by Hudson's report of the numerous whales in the northern waters.

When Hudson reported to his sponsors at the Muscovy Company of the many whales he encountered on his first voyage, they wanted him to lead a whaling expedition back to the area. Hudson refused, however, and the company financed another search for the Northwest Passage.

The company knew it could make significant financial profit from whaling. Looking to capitalize immediately, they asked Hudson to return to Whale Bay, but as the captain of a whaling expedition instead of a ship looking to find the Northwest Passage to Asia.

Hudson refused. He was an explorer, after all, and was not interested in becoming a whaling captain. He told the Muscovy Company that just because he hadn't found the passage to Asia on his first voyage of exploration it didn't mean it couldn't be found. The company again agreed to finance him on a second voyage of exploration. Throughout the winter of 1607 into 1608, Hudson prepared for his second journey.

After Hudson's report of many whales concentrated in a small area became public knowledge, the whaling frenzy began. England and other countries began sending so many ships to the Whale Bay area that it took only a decade or so to nearly exterminate all the whales in the region. Whale fishing lasted well into the twentieth century, only recently becoming challenged by environmentalists. No one actually laid a formal claim to the Svalbard Islands until the twentieth century, however, when they became Norwegian territory in 1920.

Hudson set sail from St. Katherine to the Svalbard Islands, this time with the ship's planking reinforced as a precaution against ice. It was late April 1608. The funding, once again, came from the Muscovy Company. There was a crew of fifteen on board, including Hudson's son, John, but only three other men who had been on the previous voyage. Evidently, one trip through icy northern waters had been more than enough for most. The three men who did return had faith in Hudson's ability to bring them back safely—and maybe make them rich as well. Everyone understood that there would be a great deal of wealth for anyone who could find the northern passage to Asia.

This time on board was Robert Juet, a master seaman and a man of whom Hudson commented in a letter to Hakluyt as being "filled with mean tempers." While the other members of the crew may have disagreed with the decision to include him, it seems that Juet clearly knew what he was doing, since Hudson did sign him on despite his occasionally foul mood.

A Near-Fatal Disaster

At first, the voyage seemed flawless. From April to the end of May, the *Hopewell* sailed north by northeast, reaching the northernmost tip of Norway. Hudson did, however, note in his journal, "[The weather turned] searching cold ... and then my carpenter was taken sick, and then three or four more of our company were inclining to sickness, I suppose by means of the cold." All apparently recovered, and Hudson makes no further mention of sickness.

Then, on June 9, the voyage almost ended in disaster. Bad weather and colder temperatures nearly lodged the *Hopewell* firmly into a section of ice, but Hudson guided the ship out before it became seriously damaged. He and his crew were able to break free by carefully reversing their course—no easy action with a sailing ship—and backing out, according to his journal, with several minor scrapes of the ship's exterior. After four stressful hours, they had finally broken free.

Afterward, Hudson was more cautious about keeping the *Hopewell* clear of ice, though he noted that the ship's hull again struck something that was probably a small iceberg. Other occurrences were less believable. While the next several days went without incident, Hudson noted in his journal, without any sign of it being unusual, that he and the crew had sighted a mermaid in the icy waters of the Barents Sea.

"Her skin [was] very white, and [she had] long hair hanging down behind, of [the] color black. They saw her tail, which was like the tail of a porpoise, and speckled like a mackerel," according to Hudson's journal.

Although Europeans during the Age of Exploration were learning more about the world than ever before, many still believed in such fantasies as mermaids and huge sea monsters.

MYTHICAL CREATURES

There have been many theories about what Hudson's men saw, but no clear facts have emerged. Sixteenth-century imaginations were still captured by the magic of the unknown, and traveling in the dark, icy seas, voyages where few had sailed before them, was to travel during an era in which men still believed in magical beings, such as mermaids and sea serpents.

Most explorers during Hudson's time firmly believed, for example, that unicorns could actually be found in Asia. Others were convinced that the deep ocean waters, especially those surrounding the North Pole, were home to strange sea monsters such as giant squid, octopi, and other creatures.

Other than whale and porpoise sightings, as well as a sea full of "fowls," which was the archaic way of describing fish, there were no other odd descriptions of sights for the remainder of the voyage.

Reaching the Island of Novaya Zemlya

On June 18, the *Hopewell* came to a barrier of ice on the port, or left side. They had run out of choices. Hudson ordered the ship to sail on to the southeast, and for four days the voyage continued. A week later, Hudson's crew sighted land for the first time. They had reached Nova Zembla, now known as the Russian islands of **Novaya Zemlya**. Hudson tried to sail north, but the thick ice was too limiting.

Instead, Hudson guided the *Hopewell* due south until it finally reached calm waters. Members of the crew, who probably were relieved, were sent ashore to search the land for anything that would later prove to be valuable, as well as to fill the ship's casks with freshwater. The men returned with news of fertile land, plenty of animal tracks, and, most mysterious of all, reports of two Christian crosses. Since Hudson believed Christians did not inhabit the islands, he must have been puzzled. (It's unlikely that someone who had grown up in predominantly Christian London knew that some pagan peoples also used crosses as symbols.)

Hudson was, however, more concerned with his obsession to find the northern passage. In doing so, he sent his men to watch for the local walruses on the chance that the animals might have gotten there by warmer currents—currents that would give a clue to the northern route.

There were no such hints. In July, Hudson wrote that what he had hoped would be a passage between Newland, a place he had discovered on his first voyage, and Novaya Zemlya was blocked with ice. As a result, he decided to head south, hunting for new clues to the location of another passage.

A Short Burst of Hope

That July, the *Hopewell* came upon the mouth of a wide river. Hudson described it in his journal as 6 to 9 miles (9.7 to 14.5 km) wide, twenty fathoms (120 feet) deep, with the color and taste of the sea. Its current was also very strong. Could he have found a northern passage at last?

Before Hudson could explore the river, an iceberg swept down on the waves from the north and nearly caught his vessel. The ship had been moored at the time, but it would require hours of shifting wooden beams to block and maneuver the ice around the hull to free it. At last, the *Hopewell* and its crew escaped and were free.

At that point, the crew collectively decided to return to England, but Hudson was determined to explore the river. To his disappointment, however, it grew more and more shallow. Although he was gravely disappointed, he made careful recordings of all the animal life in the region and added his conclusion that no northern passage was to be found there.

This did not mean that he had abandoned all hope of finding it. In his journal he wrote that he was still inclined to search the area for new options: "Being out of hope to find a passage by the northeast … my purpose was now to see whether Willoughby's Land is located where it is shown on our **charts**."

He then gave the order, and the *Hopewell* sailed west by southwest. There was only one problem: Although it showed up on sea charts, including the one used by Hudson, Willoughby's Land—or Willoughby's Island—did not exist. (Even though much of the world was charted by the seventeenth century, mapmakers notoriously added fantasy sketches to their maps, such was the case with what was then known as Willoughby Island.)

WILLOUGHBY
THE NORTH
53.

Henry Hudson

Willoughby Island was never found, and the ever-obsessed Hudson began feeling desperate, yet he remained charged with passion. He planned to do whatever it took to locate the Northwest Passage for England, including sailing to the New World. Unfortunately, Hudson didn't share his plans with the crew. By August, when they realized that he had no intention of returning home, they were so angry that they were most likely near mutiny.

Since there are no more entries in Hudson's journal until August 7, it is a safe assumption that his crew pressured him to return. Of this, he wrote, "I used all diligence to arrive at London, and therefore now I gave my crew a certificate under my hand, of my free and willing return, without persuasion or force . . ."

The certificate Hudson mentions in his journal was a concession to his crew that they wouldn't be charged or punished for attempted mutiny when the ship returned home. As mutineers could be hanged for their crime, it was significant insurance for the crew. When the *Hopewell* docked in England in late August, Hudson had to bring the bad news to the Muscovy Company that he has once again failed to find the Northwest Passage to Asia. Hudson was not ready to give up—he wanted to immediately begin preparation for a third voyage. However, the Muscovy Company no longer shared his enthusiasm. After spending the money to finance the first two expeditions, the company decided against any further investment in Hudson's explorations. If he was to make a third journey, he was going to need a new benefactor.

Sir Hugh Willoughby (left), like Hudson, explored the Arctic Circle and claimed to have seen an uncharted island during one of his voyages. Although mapmakers included "Willoughby Island" on their charts, it did not actually exist, causing confusion for Hudson.

Chapter 4
Sailing for the Dutch

I f Henry Hudson thought that the Muscovy Company's refusal to fund any further expeditions was a temporary setback, he soon learned otherwise. No other English company was willing to invest in a third exploration for Hudson either. Without the financial backing, Hudson

The Dutch East India Company's headquarters in Amsterdam, Netherlands. The Dutch East India Company sponsored Hudson's third voyage.

would be stranded in England, unable to make a third attempt at finding a northwest passage to Asia that obsessed him. Losing this sense of purpose frustrated Hudson, and his friends noticed a change in Hudson's demeanor. One of them, the Reverend Samuel Purchas, made a note that was eventually reprinted in Tomás Janvier's biography of the explorer, writing that Hudson "sunk into the lowest depth of . . . melancholy [depression], from which no man could rouse him."

Purchas did his best, trying to convince Hudson that the geographic information he'd brought back was a treasure and that by giving it to England he has already gained long-lasting fame. Hudson wasn't listening.

Then, in November 1608, Hudson unexpectedly received a letter from the **Dutch East India Company**, a major enterprise in the Netherlands and one that had exclusive rights to Dutch trade in Asia. The directors of the company would pay his expenses if he would come to Amsterdam to meet with them. Hudson must have been suddenly shaken out of his depression. He went to Amsterdam at once and did his best to persuade the company that he could find a successful northern passage. Some believed him, but other members of the board were skeptical. The meeting ended without the company agreeing to sponsor a new Hudson voyage.

Frustrated again, Hudson met with the Dutch geographer Petrus Plancius. Plancius also believed in a northern passage and had created a map of the world in 1594 to prove the theory that Asia could be reached by a northern sea route. They exchanged ideas in Latin—the only language they had in common—and struck up a friendship in the process. Hudson also met the engraver Jodocus Hondius, and the two men worked together on Hondius's map of the Arctic.

Unfortunately, Hudson's friendships couldn't sponsor him for the third voyage he was seeking. However, a Dutch navigator in Paris told the French king, Henry IV, about Hudson and his ideas. In response, Henry IV sent a secret envoy to meet with Hudson about the future possibility of French exploratory voyages.

Finding a New Sponsor

The meeting wasn't as secret as the French might have liked, however, and the Dutch East India Company quickly learned of it, too. They hastily reconsidered their quick denial of Hudson's plan to broaden his search. What, they may have reasoned, if he was correct after all? It made no sense to risk losing the profits that a shortcut to Asia would provide—particularly to one of their national rivals.

It was for this reason that the Dutch signed a contract with Hudson on January 8. In it, Hudson was commissioned by the company to search for another potential northern passage to Asia.

THE DUTCH EAST INDIA COMPANY

Established in 1602, the Dutch East India Company (also known as VOC, short for Verenigde Oostindische Compagnie) was one of the world's first international companies, controlling a number of shipping routes for much of the seventeenth and eighteenth centuries. The company helped the Dutch establish outposts in several countries throughout Asia, as well as an outpost on the Southern tip of Africa. Despite controlling the travel between Asia and Europe via circumnavigation of the African content, the VOC was looking for a direct route to Asia, which ultimately explained their interest in Hudson's journeys.

Did the Dutch really trust Hudson? Did they know that he had been secretly communicating with the English captain John Smith about a potential Northwest Passage? Historians believe it's possible, especially since the Dutch signed him on to specifically "think of discovering no other route or passage except the route around the north or northeast above Nova Zembla," according to a special amendment to the 1609 contract between Hudson and the Dutch East India Company.

Problems with a Mixed Crew

Hudson began preparing for the voyage and signed a crew of twenty people, including, once again, his son John. Ultimately, he gathered a mixed group of sailors, some English, some Dutch. He now had a potential problem, as not everyone spoke both languages. It didn't help matters that the English didn't think very highly of the Dutch. The foul-tempered Juet summed up the English sailors' opinions of the Dutch crew with, as it was detailed in his journal, "They are an ugly lot."

It was Juet, in his usual dark mood, who was certain that the Dutch East India Company was deliberately trying to save money by giving Hudson the oldest ship they could find. The vessel was called the *Halve Maen* (the *Half Moon*) and it was admittedly not the most modern of designs. Small and looking like a clumsy version of the *Hopewell*, it rode high in the water. This meant that it would most likely be difficult to handle in rough weather, but the company made it clear that there would be no substitution. In fact, Hudson was told that if he didn't want the *Half Moon*, they would find someone else to captain it.

Hudson accepted the commission. Then, for whatever reason, he delayed sailing from March 15 to April 6. Only portions of Hudson's journal are still available from his third voyage, since

Resembling a clumsy, clunky version of Hudson's first ship the *Hopewell*, the *Half Moon* (*Halve Maen* in Dutch) was not Hudson's ideal choice of vessel. His Dutch sponsors, however, made it clear that he would have no other choice.

his original writings were the property of his Dutch employers and were sold at public auction in 1821. And while other writings from that period are available from Juet, Hudson's mate, he used two different forms of calendars while writing it, making the dates uncertain.

With a crew composed of people who didn't understand each other, it was just a matter of time before trouble erupted. Sure enough, quarrels grew commonplace as the *Half Moon* sailed north toward Norway.

By mid May, the weather, like the moods of those aboard the ship, had turned foul. Arguments between the English and Dutch crewmen became more frequent. Hudson was hardly in the best of moods, either, since the wind was too strong to allow him to continue sailing north, not even as far as the Russian islands now known as Novaya Zemlya.

We have no way of knowing what happened next. Was it an attempt at mutiny? Was Juet behind the trouble? After nearly two weeks of wind and bad weather, Hudson changed his mind about their intended destination and decided that the time had come to sail in a southerly direction. Perhaps that had been his plan all along, since he had maps on board of the New World. His crew agreed to the change of course after Hudson promised them warmer waters and fewer storms. They put in to the Faroe Islands, west of Norway, for provisions, and then set out across the Atlantic Ocean.

If Hudson's crew had expected smoother sailing, they were mistaken. The *Half Moon* was struck by storm after storm on its way to the New World. By June 15, Juet reported in the ship's log, "We had a great storm, and [lost] overboard foremast," taking the foresail with it. It wasn't until June 19 that the weather grew calm enough for the crew to be able to improvise a temporary mast and foresail. After that, presumably to everyone's relief, they had a stretch of calm weather. On June 25, Juet noted in his journal, "We had sight of a sail and gave ... but could not speak with her."

Even though Hudson's crew spotted another vessel, they couldn't catch up with it. Why they chased it might have been, despite Juet's lack of details, not merely an attempt to speak to another crew. They might have been attempting to capture what was probably a better ship, either for booty or to rid themselves of their own creaking vessel. By 1609, it wasn't all that unlikely for a crew to spot another ship en route to the northern area of the New World. By that time, trade with the Native people, and the fishing and hunting industry were beginning, at least along the eastern coasts of what would later become Canada and the United States.

By July 2, the *Half Moon* had safely reached what is now called the Grand Banks off Newfoundland's shore, and it sailed southwest. The crew constantly sounded for depth—meaning lower-ing a weighted cable—marked regular intervals, so they could tell the depth of the water and the conditions of the sea floor below them. The last thing Hudson would have wanted to do was run aground on a **shoal** (sandbar).

Soon the crew spied a fleet of French ships. Neither Hudson nor his crew spoke with any of them. This should not be a surprise: The French, after all, were commercial rivals of both the English and the Dutch.

Reaching Land

The *Half Moon* sailed on to Newfoundland, and from there, headed farther west and south. Less than two weeks later, they were within sight of land and described a shoreline, distinctive in its showy, white sandy beaches. They were off the coast of Nova Scotia and sailed on to what is now Penobscot Bay in Maine.

Meanwhile, the weather was foggy, occasionally so much so that the crew couldn't see where they were going and had to rely on constant sounding for depth. On July 13, they sailed blindly until the late afternoon, when they again saw land and the distant sails of other ships—presumably two more of the French fishing fleet. More fog later made visibility especially poor, so Hudson had the ship's anchors lowered, and the *Half Moon* sat, waiting patiently for clearer weather. Without much else to do, the men went fishing, and Juet commented joyfully in his notes about the great wealth of cod in the ocean waters.

Finally, to everyone's relief, the weather cleared again. On July 17, Juet recounted two boats sailing out to meet them with six Native people, all seemingly pleased at Hudson's arrival near the shore.

The people native to the area were open to meeting with Hudson and his crew because they had already been trading with French explorers. Some of the Native people had even begun to learn the French language. It's fair to assume that the Native people assumed their interactions with Hudson's crew would be equally peaceful. According to Juet, the crewmen made the Native people feel even more at ease by giving them gifts and dining together. The Native people shared stories of the land's rich resources, including the presence of gold, silver, and copper in the area. If they had known of the European's interest in these metals, they may not have been so willing to share such information. The meeting was so positive that Hudson and his men decided to disembark their ship and visit the New World—the first time Hudson had ever done so.

The initial meeting between the Native Americans and Hudson's crew was friendly, and the two groups exchanged gifts and ate together.

Chapter 5

Exploring the New World

A fter so much time spent in a cramped ship at sea, the time on shore had to be a welcome respite for the crew of the *Half Moon*. They were finally able to build a replacement mast for the ship, using local timber to construct it.

Although the repair of the *Half Moon* was cause for celebration, tensions between her crew and the Native Americans were building.

Henry Hudson

They were also able to feast on local food, including thirty-one lobsters the crew managed to catch. Hudson made the meal even more festive by sharing two bottles of wine from his own store.

Juet, for one, didn't let his guard down. He recorded in his journal that the local people came aboard the *Half Moon* once again and were friendly. Still, however, he questioned their behavior, but gave no reason for his mistrust. Was it wariness, or just his usual ill humor?

Juet recorded in his journal: "Two French **shallops** [small boats] full of the country people come into the harbor. But they offered us no wrong, seeing we stood upon our guard. They brought many beaver skins and other fine furs, for which they would have changed [traded] for red gowns. For the French trade with them for red cassocks, knives, hatchets, copper, kettles . . . and other trifles."

Facing Conflict

This early friendship of the local peoples with the French would have an echo a hundred years later during the French and Indian War, when the descendants of these native people sided with the French against the British colonists.

Things were not going well between the Native people and the crew of the *Half Moon*, although we can only guess at what might have been causing the trouble. On July 24, Juet noted that he and the entire crew continued to keep watch because they feared the Native people's intentions. Days later, it seemed the brewing trouble burst into action.

A July 24 entry in Julep's journal reads: "In the morning, we manned our scute with four muskets and six men, and took one of their shallops and brought it aboard. Then we manned our boat and scute with twelve men and muskets, and two stone

Hudson was the first European to explore what is today Delaware Bay.

pieces, or murderers [small cannons]. [We] drove the [Native people] from their houses and took the spoil of them, as they would have done us."

Was there any justification for this action? We will never have the exact answer to this question, since the only account we have of what happened is that of the undeniably biased Juet. Hudson and his crew hoisted anchor and set sail again early on the morning of July 26.

By August 3, the *Half Moon* had sailed past what is now Cape Cod. Hudson had a brief moment of disappointment: Seven years before him, another captain had actually claimed what Hudson thought was new land in 1602, a place he wanted to name "New Holland." Hudson continued, and later had the satisfaction of being the first European to explore what is now Delaware Bay.

On August 4, the crew heard human voices from the shore and sent a boat to them, thinking that these might be European castaways. They turned out to be Native people, and this time, the encounter was a friendly one. They seemed genuinely happy to see the *Half Moon* crew. Juet wrote kindly of the encounter, recounting that the crew shared a meal with a man whom they soon sent back to land on one of Hudson's small boats.

Tobacco and Corn

In addition to the rich resources of the land, European explorers were also introduced to crops in the New World, particularly tobacco and corn. Tobacco leaves were one of the first gifts the Native people offered to Columbus when he landed in the New World, and the English would eventually see tobacco growing as a way to make significant profits in their Virginia colony, particularly after they did not find gold or silver in the area. Once tobacco was introduced to the European continent, there would be a consistent demand for the product that New World colonies would fill.

Corn was one of the most important crops for the Native Americans. When Europeans learned the native plant could be grown in a variety of areas, including their home continent, it became a valuable commodity.

Corn (referred to as maize by the Spanish) was a staple crop for most of the people native to North America, and they often shared the food with European explorers. Europeans found that the hearty crop could be grown in a variety of regions, and were able to bring it back to Europe more easily. The crop was treated as a commodity, and would be traded like other Old World grains, such as rye, wheat, and barley.

A man native to the area returned the favor by pointing out a river filled with lively fish. Juet and the rest of the crew observed the man's tobacco pipes of red copper. Juet was then convinced of the land's bounty. Sir John Hawkins, an English admiral and contemporary of Sir Francis Drake's, had first introduced England to the tobacco plant around 1565, but it was brought over from the New World to Europe as early as 1492.

They sailed on for the rest of August, first down to the warm South, then back north again, never finding what was still driving Hudson's obsession, the elusive passage to Asia.

By September, the *Half Moon* had reached what is now Lower New York Bay, anchoring near modern-day Sandy Hook, New Jersey. Chances are that Hudson and his crew were pleased with the sights and condition of the land. Juet recorded in the ship's log that the terrain was good enough to settle, certainly bountiful, and able to sustain a larger population. He was even taken with the landscape and called it "pleasant." As they lowered anchor, they came upon members of a branch of the Algonquian group of Native tribes. Hudson was probably relieved to see that they were friendly. The group greeted Hudson and his crew and exchanged tobacco leaves for some of the *Half Moon*'s knives and other trinkets. Among the new food Hudson tasted was corn. Not knowing what type of plant it was, he called it Turkish wheat. Later, Juet began referring to it as "Indian wheat." Juet, predictably, remained ill at ease.

Losing a Crew Member

As it turned out, Juet wasn't wrong about being wary. Hudson sent five of his men, led by John Colman, who'd been with Hudson on his first voyage, to explore another river. Yet as the five men sailed upriver, Native warriors attacked them without warning. Colman was slain instantly by an arrow through the throat, while two other men in the group were wounded. The survivors fled downriver, where they spent a terrifying night, unable to find the *Half Moon* in the darkness.

In the morning they recovered, and Colman's body was buried. The *Half Moon* remained at anchor through the night, and Hudson ordered a careful watch kept. There was no further sign of trouble, though. To Hudson and the rest of the crew, it was plain enough: All the Native people were now suspect, or could not be trusted.

Other local people came to trade with the *Half Moon* the following day, September 8, as though nothing had happened. Juet wrote about the dealings, which made no mention of Colman or the fact that he had been killed two days before.

Hudson and his crew were still worried. On September 9, matters came to a head. Juet wrote that two canoes full of men met the *Half Moon*, each with his bow and arrow showing, while others held knives. Subsequently, two Native men were taken as hostages by the English crew.

Unfortunately for Hudson, both hostages escaped. Hudson, who wrote in his journal, "Had they indicated by a cunning light in their eyes that they had knowledge of the foul murder, I was prepared . . . to exterminate all." He ordered the *Half Moon* moved to a safer distance inside the bay, now Upper New York Bay, or New York Harbor, anchoring overnight near the tip of the island now known as Manhattan.

However, the Native people followed.

On the morning of September 12, twenty-eight canoes paddled out to meet the *Half Moon*. The ever-wary Juet wrote in the log that they were full of Native people—men, women, and children—all intending to attack the English crew. Juet didn't realize that it would have been unlikely that warriors would take women and children with them to institute a conflict. Although the Native people weren't allowed on board, they still managed to sell the crew some oysters and beans. In return for their trouble, Hudson took two of them hostage.

Resuming the Search for the Passage

The canoes departed by midday, and Hudson then ordered his crew to continue sailing north, up into the wide tidal river that now bears his name. Although Italian and Portuguese explorers had explored the river's mouth before; no one had yet explored the river itself, which spans 2 miles (3.2 km) at its widest point. Hudson proudly claimed the entire region, now known as the Hudson River Valley, for his employers, the Dutch East India Company.

By the time the *Half Moon* had reached what is now Yonkers, Hudson had become hopeful that this, at last, was the passage to Asia. Considering the river's length and width, it's easy to see why he thought he had finally found the Northwest Passage. By September 15, the ship had reached the widest point of the Hudson, near where the Tappan Zee Bridge crosses it today, and it appeared to be a promising course to Arctic waters. Soon after, however, it began to narrow again and grow shallower. By the time they had reached what would one day be Albany, there was no longer any doubt that this was merely another river.

Adding to Hudson's discouragement, the two hostages escaped the following day, September 15, slipping through a porthole and swimming ashore, then yelling taunts back at the *Half Moon* and its crew. That night, things grew a little brighter, though. Juet recounted meeting other Native people without wariness, individuals who intended no harm to the English crew.

By September 17, Hudson proved to himself without doubt that he had not, in fact, located a northern passage to Asia. The river grew so shallow that the *Half Moon* ran aground. Fortunately, since the Hudson is a tidal river, a waterway that allows the entrance of seawater to mix with fresh, unsalted waters, high tide was just enough to float the vessel free again. As far as the Native people were concerned, it seemed as though Hudson and his crew had finally established a mutual level of trust between them.

"[Me and my first mate] determined to try some of the chief men of the country [to see] whether they had any treachery in them," Hudson wrote in his journal. "So they took them down into the cabin [of the *Half Moon*], and gave them so much wine … that they were all merry. One of them had his wife with them, [who] sat so modestly as any of our countrywomen would do in a strange place. In the end, one of them was drunk ... and that was strange to them."

The man who had gotten drunk slept the night aboard the *Half Moon*, and in the morning was returned to his people. They were relieved to see him unharmed, as was Hudson to witness the lack of hostility. Hudson's good humor soon fled, for he had to accept that there was no chance of sailing any farther north. At last, the *Half Moon* had to turn back.

An Unexpected Ambush

Soon trouble found them again. By October, more Native people boarded the ship, and examined it and the crew's weapons. All seemed well, but soon one man lingering in a canoe, hanging about listlessly, slipped silently on board and attempted to steal some clothing and weapons. He was surprised by the first mate, who abruptly shot and killed him. Another man tried to climb into the boat too, but the ship's cook killed him with a sword. Hudson ordered the anchor raised, and the *Half Moon* sailed downriver.

By the next day, the *Half Moon* had gone 20 miles (32 km) south. As the ship neared the island of Manhattan, canoes bearing at least a hundred angry warriors ambushed it. Arrows whizzed through the air, and shots rang out from the *Half Moon*. In the end, the vessel got away without the loss of English lives, but several Native warriors died.

For Hudson and his crew, the battles had taken their toll— he decided to return to Europe. The *Half Moon* made its way home in November, but Hudson decided to dock in England. In a letter to his employers at the Dutch East India Company, Hudson wrote that he wanted to continue to search for the Northwest Passage to Asia, and that after winter ended, he'd like to set sail again in the spring of 1610. The company first demanded that Hudson return the ship to them before deciding on how to proceed.

This request would prove problematic. The English were upset that Hudson had been exploring for another country, and so they seized the ship and arrested Hudson, charging him with "voyaging to the detriment of his country."

Chapter 6

The Fourth and Final Voyage

It is unclear why Hudson was arrested for working for the Dutch. He was not the first English explorer to work for a foreign country, and yet these other men had not stood trial for the same activity. There's little doubt that while Hudson was docked that news of his voyage and

Hudson's fourth and final voyage would be met with tragedy.

the potential for rich rewards in the New World made its way around the city. Some have speculated that jealous merchants or rival captains pushed for Hudson to be arrested. He and his crew were brought before the king, and Hudson was ordered to never sail on the behalf of a foreign power again.

Hudson's imprisonment, which turned out to be on a minor charge, did not last long. Not only was he set free just days later, he also made a deal with another company—The English East India Company, a direct rival of his previous employers, as well as the Muscovy Company. The company agreed to sponsor a fourth voyage in search of the Northwest Passage and, not incidentally, for any gold or other valuable minerals along the way. This quick dismissal and new charter adds credence to the idea that the charges against Hudson were more about ensuring that any new discoveries Hudson made were for English companies. His next chance to search for the Northwest Passage would be as captain of the English ship *Discovery*. It was a sturdy vessel, larger and in better shape than his previous commands. The *Half Moon* had been returned to the Dutch and sunk not long after.

Setting out on the *Discovery*

On April 17, 1610, the *Discovery* set sail with a crew of twenty-two men that again included Hudson's son John and the still bitter-minded Juet. For this fourth voyage, only a partial account from Hudson remains, but a more complete account was kept by another member of the fateful crew, Abacuk Prickett.

Hudson, still in English waters, stated in his journal on April 22 that he put one of the crew, a Master Coleburne, off the ship in a pinkie (small boat) bound for London, while moored at Lee. This may have been because he was a company man, there to keep an eye on the English East India Company's investment.

Hudson wouldn't have wanted someone watching his every move. To replace him, and without telling his employers, Hudson took on Henry Greene at Gravesend, a man he had known in London. Unfortunately, Hudson may not have known that Greene also had a reputation as a gambler and troublemaker.

There was little trouble through the month of May, though. The crew sighted Iceland by May 11 and witnessed the eruption of the Icelandic volcano Mount Hekla. While Hudson didn't mention it, Prickett recounted the lively event in his journal, writing how the crew saw the famous hill casting out a great fire, a sign that he believed would certainly bring bad weather for the journey.

Difficulties on the *Discovery*

This also marked the beginning of trouble aboard the *Discovery*. A few days afterward, Henry Greene argued with Edward Wilson, the ship's surgeon, and a fistfight ensued. Hudson broke it up, taking Greene's side, while the crew sided with Wilson. There were uneasy feelings all around. Hudson later wrote in his journal that Wilson "had a tongue that would wrong his best friend."

About the only pleasant part of their voyage past Iceland was the chance the men had to bathe in one of the island's geothermal pools, which, as Prickett noted in his journal, had waters that were hot enough "to scorch the region's fowl."

By June 1, the *Discovery* was on its way to Greenland. Yet when they reached it three days later, Hudson and his crew found there was too much ice to let them draw close. Instead, Hudson headed the *Discovery* southwest until there was some clear sailing up to the northwest again on June 15. It still wasn't completely clear.

The *Discovery* had a narrow run-in with a pod of whales. Prickett described in the ship's log what could have been a disaster. At least three whales came so close to the ship they could hardly be avoided. One whale even passed under the vessel, causing greater alarm. The *Discovery* could very well have been overturned by something as large as a whale if the animal had surfaced just then, but Prickett added that the stability of the vessel had returned to normal in the frigid waters.

Navigating the Ice

By June 21, the *Discovery* had reached what is now the coast of Labrador, but again it ran into ice. For three days, the sailing was slow, though they did catch a glimpse of Resolution Island on June 24, but just as swiftly they lost sight of it. Hudson ordered them to continue sailing due west.

Four days later, the *Discovery* reached what is now called Hudson Strait, part of Canada, between northern Quebec Province and Baffin Island. There was ice as far as the eye could see. Hudson had no way of knowing that the strait was dangerous because of icebergs until the middle of July. Instead, the *Discovery*, pressed by winds, was again forced south, blocked by ice from getting near any shore.

By the beginning of July, Prickett noted in his journal, "Some of our men … fell sick. I will not say it was for fear, though I saw small signs of other grief." By this he meant that discontent was rising among the crew. Hudson, however, did not seem to have noticed the dissatisfaction among the crewmen. He wrote nothing of it in his journal.

He did notice that on July 6 and 7, there seemed to be ice blocking them from ever sailing farther west. The *Discovery* sailed into a bay but got nowhere. Prickett painted a dramatic picture in his journal.

"Into the current we went and made our way [north by northwest] till we met with ice. Wherefore our master … cleared himself of this ice and stood [steered] to the south, than the west, through the store of floating ice. We gained a clear sea … till we met with more ice, first with great islands, then with store of the smaller sort. Between them, we made our course northwest, till we met with ice again. We saw one of the great islands of ice overturn, which was a good warning to us … The next day we had a storm, and the wind brought the ice fast upon us. Our course was as the ice did lie, sometimes to the north, then to the northwest, then to the west, and then to the southwest, but still enclosed with ice. The more [Hudson] strove, the worse he was."

By this time, even Hudson was in despair. He confessed to Prickett that he was certain they were never going to get out of the ice and that they would die there.

The crew, understandably, wasn't any happier. They probably would have mutinied then and there if that had gotten them home. However, Hudson, who might have been unable to think of anything else to say, proudly displayed his charts to show the crew that they had sailed farther west than any Englishmen ever had before. He left the choice to them: Should they continue or not?

There was no real choice then but to work the ship free of ice. At last they managed to maneuver the *Discovery* loose, and Hudson insisted on continuing the journey.

In the days that followed, from July 8 until the end of the month, the *Discovery* continued west and followed a pattern of avoiding icebergs, anchoring to ride out storms, and exploring island after barren island. Once, the men attempted to shoot a polar bear, but it escaped over the loose ice floes. The *Discovery* was nearly caught in what is now Ungava Bay in Canada, but the crew managed to edge their way along the shore of the bay and out into open sea again, this time headed northwest. Hudson mapped and named all the islands they found, usually after English royalty, but by this point, the crew probably didn't care what he named them.

THE HUDSON BAY COMPANY

The Hudson Bay Company later explored the North American and Canadian region and set up quite a trading empire in the eighteenth and nineteenth centuries. The company still exists. A full-scale replica of its sailing ship *Nonsuch* was built and sailed the coast of England, the Great Lakes, and the Pacific Northwest before being assigned a permanent home in the Manitoba Museum of Man and Nature in Winnipeg, Canada. Hudson Bay blankets made of heavy wool can still be bought from Canada, and the company runs a Canadian chain of department stores which are called simply the Bay.

Then, at the beginning of August, Hudson wrote that they had finally sailed into a great expanse of water. He and his crew had entered what is now Hudson Bay.

Soon the *Discovery* came across a deep inlet flowing into the sea from the northwest. Hudson ordered the crew to sail into it.

Along the way, they stopped on an island covered with nesting seabirds and remarked about its beautiful grasses and rounded hills of stone, which they believed were made by the hands of Christians. What they had really found were some Inuit cairns being used to cure duck meat.

Hudson was in no mood for dallying, even though Prickett, among others, asked for more time, a day or two, to recover in this unexpectedly pleasant place. Hudson insisted that they all return to the *Discovery* at once. Prickett noted in his journal that Hudson refused to remain there, still obsessed by his mission.

This was another mistake on Hudson's part. His men would have been a great deal more agreeable to his ideas if he had allowed them a brief vacation. Hudson insisted that they all keep sailing—which added to a disagreeable crew.

A Mutinous Crew

The *Discovery* continued exploring islands. The crew took to arguing among themselves, and finally with Hudson, over what direction to take. At last, on September 10, matters came to a head for the first—but not the last—time. Sour-tongued Juet got into a battle of words with his captain, and Hudson had definitely had enough. Hudson ordered a shipboard trial of Juet for mutiny. We have the account written in the ship's log by crewmember Thomas Woodhouse, who described how Hudson let Juet speak for himself. "There were proved so many and great abuses, and mutinous matters" that Juet had raised that "it was fit time to punish and cut off farther occasions of the like mutinies," according to the account log.

Things quickly worsened. The *Discovery* spent the month of October aimlessly wandering through Hudson Bay, going northwest, north and then south again, and finally east. It was as though Hudson had finally given up on finding what he sought. By the end of October, there was no doubt in his mind that they were going to have to settle down for the winter. The crew managed to haul the ship aground, and they did what they could to survive the dark and freezing cold of the subarctic temperatures. Prickett wrote in his journal, "to speak of all our trouble would be too tedious."

Hudson seemed to have lost control, getting into arguments

Hudson Bay. Hudson's crew grew disgruntled after months of sailing around the harsh waters of the Canadian Arctic.

with the crew over matters he should have been able to settle. In one case, he gave a dead crewman's cloak to another crewman instead of following the custom of auctioning it off to provide the dead man's next of kin with money. Hudson also shouted at men over small matters using foul, even profane, language. He also fought with the man he had brought aboard, treacherous Henry Greene, who, as Prickett wrote, attempted to discredit and humiliate his position as captain.

Until the end of November, the men were able to catch and kill enough birds to keep them alive. Then the birds went south, and the crew was reduced to eating frogs and even moss, and treating **scurvy**, a disease brought about by vitamin C deficiency, with a natural medicine. There was a visit from one local tribesman, but after a brief meeting with the desperate Hudson, the man left and never returned.

Hudson's Final Mistakes

As the winter turned slowly into spring, the men were able to catch about 500 small fish and rejoiced. However, that many fish would not be found again. By the middle of May 1611, Greene had convinced some to leave the *Discovery* and fend for themselves, but they were dismayed when they ran into a hostile tribe who set the forest on fire before they could make any approach.

At last the brief northern spring warmed the waters enough so that the *Discovery* could be re-launched. Hudson, weeping, doled out what remained of the food and water. There should, according to the listing, have been nine cheeses on board, but Hudson showed only five. Greene promptly claimed that he was holding back provisions. Hudson retorted that the remaining foods were far too spoiled for eating. The crew was certain that they were finally going home. Hudson instead ordered the ship to be sailed west, and he even went so far as to have the crew's gear searched for hoarded bread. That was his final mistake.

On May 22, the mutiny began. Led by Henry Greene, with Juet assisting, the mutineers seized Hudson, his son, and approximately six other sickly crewmembers who still supported him, cast them off the *Discovery* into a small boat, and abandoned them.

That was the last anyone ever saw of the explorer Henry Hudson. Most of the mutineers, including Juet, died on the long journey back to England. In September, only six men remained. They were rescued by a fishing boat. They had been away from England for nearly a year and a half.

In October, the mutineers were questioned, but a formal trial was postponed until 1618. By then, those who survived after so long were found not guilty and were set free.

Katherine Hudson did her best to persuade the Dutch East India Company to send out a rescue party for her husband. It took her three long years, but at last they sent out a ship. It found no trace of the doomed explorer. Officially widowed, Katherine sought compensation for the loss of her husband to the point where the company directors began referring to her as "that troublesome and impatient woman" in their records. However, she won the case. Katherine Hudson even forced the English East India Company to fund her journey to India, where she purchased indigo, a valuable dye. Showing a strong head for business, she returned from her travels a wealthy woman who was even received at the royal court. She died in 1624, leaving everything to her two surviving sons, Richard and Oliver.

While Henry Hudson never achieved his singular life goal, he is still considered a key figure in both the northeastern United States and Canada as well, with both a river and bay named after him. Hudson traveled farther north and west than any previous European explorers. His charts and journals enabled the Dutch to establish a presence in New York, including the founding of what is today New York City.

Hudson's mutinous crew set him, his son, and six other crewmembers adrift in the frigid arctic waters of Hudson Bay. Not one of them was seen again.

Timeline

1553

Sir Hugh Willoughby perishes while searching for the northern passage to Asia

1555

The Muscovy Company is formed to establish trade with Russia

1556

Stephen Burrough navigates to the entrance of the Kara Sea

1558

Queen Elizabeth I comes into power

Circa 1565

Henry Hudson is born in England

1576

Martin Frobisher sails north through Frobisher Bay and reaches Baffin Island

1577

Sir Francis Drake circumnavigates the globe

1582

Richard Hakluyt publishes his first book, *Diverse Voyages Touching the Discovery of America*

1585

John Davis's first northern voyage

1595

First Dutch voyage to the Far East

1600

Hakluyt publishes *The Principal Navigations*

1602

Formation of the Dutch East India Company

1607

Founding of Jamestown by the Virginia Company;
Henry Hudson, on the *Hopewell*, makes his first
voyage to find the Northwest Passage to Asia for the
Muscovy Company

1608

Henry Hudson searches for the Northwest Passage for
the Dutch East India Company

1609

Hudson explores present-day New York

1610

Hudson explores Hudson Bay

1611

Mutiny aboard the *Discovery*; Henry Hudson disappears
after he is set adrift in a small boat

1624

The Dutch settle Manhattan Island

1631

Luke Foxe and Thomas James make the last attempt to
find the Northwest Passage during the Age of Exploration

Glossary

astrolabe A medieval instrument used to determine the altitude of the sun or other celestial bodies.

cabin boy A boy servant aboard a ship.

carrack A type of merchant ship used between the fourteenth and sixteenth centuries; a galleon.

chart A map of maritime and coastal areas used by sailors to navigate.

circumnavigate To go or travel completely around, especially by water.

cross staff An early sixteenth-century instrument for measuring the altitude of a heavenly body.

Dutch East India Company Considered the first multinational corporation in the world, the Dutch East India Company was a powerful business chartered in the seventeenth century by the Dutch government to perform all colonial activities in Asia, including establish new trade routes to the continent.

Elizabethan Era Relating to the time during the reign of England's Queen Elizabeth I (1558–1603).

log A ship's official record of events during its voyage.

mutiny Open rebellion against constituted authority.

Northwest Passage A sea route along the coast of North America connecting the Atlantic and Pacific oceans. Early explorers thought that a westward route would facilitate trade with wealthy Asian countries, which at the time could only be reached by long, costly, and potentially dangerous easterly routes.

Novaya Zemlya (Nova Zembla) Islands situated off the northern coast of Russia.

prow The forward part of a ship's hull; the bow.

quadrant An early instrument for measuring altitude, consisting of a ninety-degree graduated arc with a moveable radius for measuring angles.

scurvy A disease caused by a deficiency of vitamin C with symptoms that include nausea, weakness, loss of hair and teeth, and eventually death. Scurvy was the most prevalent cause of death among sailors between the fifteenth and seventeenth centuries.

shallop An open boat fitted with oars, sails, or both.

shoal A sandy elevation of the bottom of a body of water, constituting a hazard to navigation; a sandbank or sandbar.

steer To guide a vessel by means of a device such as a rudder, paddle, or wheel.

stern The rear portion of a ship.

sterncastle A two-story cabin on a sailing vessel.

For More Information

Books

Butts, Edward. *Henry Hudson: New World Voyager.* Toronto, ON: Dundurn Press, 2012.

Hunter, Douglas. *Half Moon: Henry Hudson and the Voyage That Redrew the Map of the New World.* New York, NY: Bloomsbury Press, 2009.

Weaver, Janie. *Hudson.* New York, NY: Random House, 2011.

Williams, Glyn. *Arctic Labyrinth: The Quest for the Northwest Passage.* Berkeley, CA: University of California Press, 2010.

Websites

Empire of the Bay

www.pbs.org/empireofthebay/profiles/hudson.html#

PBS's webpage for its *Empire of the Bay* broadcast features a biography of Henry Hudson's life, illustrations, quizzes, an interactive timeline, and transcripts of the broadcast.

The History Channel's Henry Hudson Page

www.history.com/topics/henry-hudson

Learn more about Hudson and his multiple attempts to find the fabled Northwest Passage.

The Mariner's Museum: Henry Hudson

ageofex.marinersmuseum.org/index.php?type=explorer&id=15

This website offers a detailed biography of Henry Hudson, accounts of his voyages, illustrations of Hudson and his ships, and an interactive map.

Index